Halloween Cookbook for Kids

Spooky, Simple, and Fun Recipes Kids Can Cook, Share, and Enjoy This Halloween

BY: SHARON B. JONES

TABLE OF CONTENTS

Halloween Cookbook for Kids i

1. Monster Cheese Quesadillas...4
2. Witch's Fingers (Carrot Snacks)...4
3. Mummy Hot Dogs 4
4. Monster Apple Mouths...4
5. Banana Ghost Pops 5
6. Carrot Finger Sticks 5
7. Spooky Veggie Platter 5
8. Jack-o'-Lantern Oranges 5
9. Cucumber Coffin Sandwiches 6
10. Cauliflower Ghost Bites...6
11. Eyeball Meatball Skewers 6
12. Spider Web Quesadillas...6
13. Jack-o'-Lantern Cheese Toast 7
14. Mummy Hot Dogs 7
15. Vampire Bite Bagels 7
16. Pumpkin Face Sliders 7
17. Boo-tiful Mac & Cheese Cups..8
18. Ghoul Grilled Cheese 8
19. Spooky Sausage Fingers 8
20. Monster Cheese Quesadillas (Variation).......................8
21. Ghostly Popcorn Balls 9
22. Monster Eyeball Cookies..9
23. Pumpkin Patch Veggie Cups..9
24. Spider Crackers 9
25. Jack-o'-Lantern Cheese Balls..10
26. Creepy Cucumber Cups 10
27. Bat Wings Chicken Nuggets 10
28. Witch Hat Cookies 10
29. Monster Veggie Wraps 11
30. Eyeball Deviled Eggs 11
31. Pumpkin Spice Muffins 11
32. Monster Rice Krispie Treats 11
33. Mummy Brownies 12
34. Ghost Banana Smoothies 12
35. Eyeball Pasta 12
36. Pumpkin Deviled Eggs 12
37. Witch Finger Cookies 13
38. Candy Corn Parfaits 13
39. Spider Mini Pizzas 13
40. Monster Fruit Cups 13
41. Mini Pumpkin Pies...14
42. Spooky Pretzel Sticks..14
43. Monster Smoothie Bowls...14
44. Witch Hat Brownies 14
45. Jack-o'-Lantern Toast 15
46. Spooky Veggie Dip Cups..15
47. Ghostly Cheese Quesadillas 15
48. Creepy Crawly Trail Mix 15
49. Spooky Apple Monsters 16
50. Bat Wing Chicken Bites 16
51. Vampire Bite Tacos 16
52. Zombie Finger Sandwiches 16
53. Haunted Hash Browns 17
54. Eyeball Spaghetti...17
55. Jack-o'-Lantern Stuffed Peppers 17
56. Bat Wing Chicken Bites 17
57. Spooky Shepherd's Pie 18
58. Eyeball Pizza 18
59. Monster Macaroni Bake...18
60. Ghostly Tomato Soup..18
61. Spider Web Pancakes 19
62. Mummy Calzones...19
63. Pumpkin Pancakes 19
64. Monster Cheese Toasties...19
65. Ghostly Pudding Cups 20
66. Witch's Cauldron Chili...20
67. Candy Corn Rice Krispie Treats 20
68. Monster Veggie Skewers..20
69. Ghostly Garlic Bread 21
70. Pumpkin Spice Smoothie 21
71. Monster Nachos...21
72. Witch Finger Pretzels 21
73. Pumpkin Rice Pudding 22

74. Monster Apple Pops 22
75. Ghostly Donuts 22
76. Spooky Jello Cups 22
77. Candy Corn Parfaits 23
78. Mini Jack-o'-Lantern Pies 23
79. Spooky Halloween Cake Pops 23
80. Graveyard Dirt Cups 23
81. Spiderweb Taco Dip 24
82. Monster Cupcakes 24
83. Ghostly Cheese Balls 24
84. Pumpkin Pie Smoothie 24
85. Mummy Cheese Sticks 25
86. Witch Hat Cupcakes 25
87. Pumpkin Cheesecake Bites 25
88. Creepy Crawly Trail Mix 25
89. Eyeball Punch 26
90. Monster Fruit Kabobs 26
91. Vampire Cupcakes 26
92. Mummy Pretzel Rods 26
93. Eyeball Pancakes 27
94. Ghostly Marshmallow Pops 27
95. Jack-o'-Lantern Quesadillas 27
96. Witch's Brew Smoothie 27
97. Monster Cheese Crackers 28
98. Pumpkin Patch Cupcakes 28
99. Ghostly Fruit Cups 28
100. Graveyard Chocolate Pudding 28

RECIPES

1. Monster Cheese Quesadillas

Cook Time: 10 minutes
Prep Time: 5 minutes
Total Time: 15 minutes

Ingredients:
- 2 large flour tortillas
- 1 cup shredded cheddar cheese
- 6 black olive slices (for eyes)
- Salsa (optional)

INSTRUCTIONS:

1. Put the tortilla over medium heat in a nonstick skillet.
2. Evenly distribute cheese on top of the tortilla.
3. When the second tortilla is golden brown and the cheese has melted, fry it for two to three minutes on each side.
4. Cut into "monster teeth" triangular shapes.
5. Serve with salsa and garnish with olive slices for eyes.

Nutrition (per serving): ~250 cal | 10g protein | 12g fat | 28g carbs

2. Witch's Fingers (Carrot Snacks)

Cook Time: 5 minutes
Prep Time: 5 minutes
Total Time: 10 minutes

Ingredients:
- 6 large carrots
- 6 almond slices (fingernails)
- Hummus (optional for dipping)

INSTRUCTIONS:

1. Cut carrots into finger-sized pieces after peeling them.
2. To make it look like a fingernail, place a piece of almond on the tip.
3. Serve as a "witch finger" snack with hummus.

Nutrition (per finger): ~25 cal | 1g protein | 1g fat | 4g carbs

3. Mummy Hot Dogs

Cook Time: 15 minutes
Prep Time: 5 minutes
Total Time: 20 minutes

Ingredients:
- 6 hot dogs
- 1 can crescent roll dough
- Mustard or ketchup for eyes

INSTRUCTIONS:

1. Turn the oven on to 375°F, or 190°C.
2. Slice the dough for the crescent rolls into thin pieces.
3. To give each hot dog a mummy appearance, lightly wrap it in strips of dough.
4. Bake until golden, 12 to 15 minutes.
5. For the eyes, add ketchup or mustard dots.

Nutrition (per mummy): ~180 cal | 6g protein | 9g fat | 17g carbs

4. Monster Apple Mouths

Cook Time: 10 minutes
Prep Time: 5 minutes
Total Time: 15 minutes

Ingredients:
- 3 apples, cored and sliced into wedges
- 6 tbsp peanut butter or almond butter
- 12 mini marshmallows (teeth)
- 6 grape halves (tongue)

INSTRUCTIONS:

1. Spread apple wedges with peanut butter.
2. Put little marshmallows for teeth along the edge.
3. For the tongue, add a grape half.
4. Serve right away.

Nutrition (per monster mouth): ~100 cal | 2g protein | 3g fat | 18g carbs

5. Banana Ghost Pops

Cook Time: 15 minutes
Prep Time: 5 minutes
Total Time: 20 minutes

Ingredients:
- 3 bananas, cut in half
- 6 popsicle sticks
- ½ cup white chocolate melts
- Mini chocolate chips (eyes and mouth)

INSTRUCTIONS:

1. Put popsicle sticks into the halves of bananas.
2. Dip bananas in white chocolate that has melted.
3. To make ghost faces, add chocolate chips.
4. Ten minutes before serving, freeze.

Nutrition (per ghost): ~80 cal | 1g protein | 2g fat | 18g carbs

6. Carrot Finger Sticks

Cook Time: 5 minutes
Prep Time: 5 minutes
Total Time: 10 minutes

Ingredients:
- 6 large carrots, cut into sticks
- 12 almond slices (fingernails)
- Hummus (optional for dipping)

INSTRUCTIONS:

1. Put a sliver of almond on the fingernail end of the carrot stick.
2. Serve with hummus.

Nutrition (per finger): ~25 cal | 1g protein | 1g fat | 4g carbs

7. Spooky Veggie Platter

Cook Time: 10 minutes
Prep Time: 5 minutes
Total Time: 15 minutes

Ingredients:
- 1 cup cherry tomatoes
- 1 cup cucumber slices
- 1 cup bell pepper strips
- ½ cup ranch or yogurt dip
- Olive slices (eyes for monster faces)

INSTRUCTIONS:

1. Put vegetables in creative Halloween shapes.
2. Slices of olive oil can be used as eyes.
3. Serve with dip.

Nutrition (per serving): ~60 cal | 2g protein | 2g fat | 10g carbs

8. Jack-o'-Lantern Oranges

Cook Time: 5 minutes
Prep Time: 2 minutes
Total Time: 7 minutes

Ingredients:
- 6 small oranges or clementines
- Black edible marker or food-safe pen

INSTRUCTIONS:

1. Directly draw jack-o'-lantern faces on oranges.
2. Serve whole or cut into "pumpkin slices" by peeling.

Nutrition (per orange): ~60 cal | 1g protein | 0g fat | 15g carbs

9. Cucumber Coffin Sandwiches

Cook Time: 10 minutes
Prep Time: 5 minutes
Total Time: 15 minutes

Ingredients:
- 1 cucumber, sliced lengthwise into thin planks
- 4 oz cream cheese
- 6 mini cherry tomatoes, halved

INSTRUCTIONS:

1. Spread slices of cucumber with cream cheese.
2. To decorate the coffin, place cherry tomato halves on top.

Nutrition (per sandwich): ~35 cal | 1g protein | 2g fat | 4g carbs

10. Cauliflower Ghost Bites

Cook Time: 15 minutes
Prep Time: 5 minutes
Total Time: 20 minutes

Ingredients:
- 2 cups cauliflower florets
- 1 tbsp olive oil
- Salt & pepper
- 12 mini chocolate chips (optional for ghost faces)

INSTRUCTIONS:

1. Turn the oven on to 400°F, or 200°C.
2. Add salt, pepper, and olive oil to the cauliflower.
3. Bake for 12 to 15 minutes, or until brown and soft.
4. Chocolate chips for ghost faces are optional.

Nutrition (per bite): ~20 cal | 1g protein | 1g fat | 4g carbs

11. Eyeball Meatball Skewers

Cook Time: 15 minutes
Prep Time: 10 minutes
Total Time: 25 minutes

Ingredients:
- 12 small cooked meatballs
- 6 mozzarella balls (bocconcini)
- 6 black olives, sliced
- Toothpicks or skewers

INSTRUCTIONS:

1. Put a mozzarella ball and a meatball on each skewer.
2. To make the "eyeball," place a slice of olive on top of the mozzarella.
3. Serve cold or warm.

Nutrition (per skewer): ~130 cal | 7g protein | 6g fat | 8g carbs

12. Spider Web Quesadillas

Cook Time: 10 minutes
Prep Time: 5 minutes
Total Time: 15 minutes

Ingredients:
- 4 large flour tortillas
- 1 cup shredded cheddar cheese
- Salsa (optional)

INSTRUCTIONS:

1. Evenly spread one tortilla with cheese, then cover with another tortilla.
2. Cook in a pan over medium heat for 2 to 3 minutes on each side, or until brown and the cheese has melted.
3. Cut into triangles and cover with a web-like design of sour cream.
4. Serve with salsa.

Nutrition (per quesadilla): ~200 cal | 8g protein | 10g fat | 20g carbs

13. Jack-o'-Lantern Cheese Toast

Cook Time: 5 minutes
Prep Time: 5 minutes
Total Time: 10 minutes

Ingredients:
- 4 slices bread
- 4 tbsp cream cheese
- ½ cup shredded cheddar cheese
- Olive slices (eyes)
- Red pepper or tomato (mouth)

INSTRUCTIONS:

1. Spread cream cheese on the barely toasted bread.
2. Top with a dollop of cheddar cheese.
3. Jack-o'-lantern faces may be made with peppers and olives.
4. Bake at 350°F (175°C) for 5 to 7 minutes, or until the cheese is melted.

Nutrition (per toast): ~160 cal | 6g protein | 8g fat | 15g carbs

14. Mummy Hot Dogs

Cook Time: 15 minutes
Prep Time: 5 minutes
Total Time: 20 minutes

Ingredients:
- 6 hot dogs
- 1 can crescent roll dough
- Mustard or ketchup for eyes

INSTRUCTIONS:

1. Turn the oven on to 375°F, or 190°C.
2. To make hot dogs look like mummies, wrap them gently in strips of dough.
3. Bake until golden, 12 to 15 minutes.
4. For the eyes, add ketchup or mustard dots.

Nutrition (per mummy): ~180 cal | 6g protein | 9g fat | 17g carbs

15. Vampire Bite Bagels

Cook Time: 5 minutes
Prep Time: 5 minutes
Total Time: 10 minutes

Ingredients:
- 4 mini bagels, halved
- 4 tbsp cream cheese
- 8 almond slices (fangs)
- 4 grape halves (blood)

INSTRUCTIONS:

1. Cover bagels with cream cheese.
2. At one edge, arrange the almond slices for the fangs.
3. For "blood," add a half of a grape.

Nutrition (per bagel): ~200 cal | 7g protein | 6g fat | 30g carbs

16. Pumpkin Face Sliders

Cook Time: 15 minutes
Prep Time: 5 minutes
Total Time: 20 minutes

Ingredients:
- 6 slider buns
- 6 mini beef patties
- 6 cheese slices
- Ketchup and mustard for decoration

INSTRUCTIONS:

1. Place cooked patties with cheese on buns.
2. You can make pumpkin faces on cheese with ketchup and mustard.

Nutrition (per slider): ~220 cal | 12g protein | 10g fat | 18g carbs

17. Boo-tiful Mac & Cheese Cups

Cook Time: 12 minutes
Prep Time: 10 minutes
Total Time: 22 minutes

Ingredients:
- 2 cups cooked macaroni
- 1 cup shredded cheddar cheese
- ½ cup milk
- 6 mini muffin liners

INSTRUCTIONS:
1. Combine milk, cheese, and macaroni.
2. Fill muffin liners with the mixture.
3. Bake at 350°F (175°C) for 10 to 12 minutes.
4. Adding tiny olive slices for ghost eyes is optional.

Nutrition (per cup): ~180 cal | 8g protein | 6g fat | 22g carbs

18. Ghoul Grilled Cheese

Cook Time: 5 minutes
Prep Time: 5 minutes
Total Time: 10 minutes

Ingredients:
- 4 slices bread
- 4 slices cheddar cheese
- Olive slices (eyes)

INSTRUCTIONS:
1. Prepare sandwiches with grilled cheese as usual.
2. Slices of olive are added for the ghost eyes.

Nutrition (per sandwich): ~200 cal | 10g protein | 10g fat | 20g carbs

19. Spooky Sausage Fingers

Cook Time: 15 minutes
Prep Time: 5 minutes
Total Time: 20 minutes

Ingredients:
- 6 sausages
- 6 hot dog buns
- 6 almond slices (fingernails)
- Ketchup (optional)

INSTRUCTIONS:
1. Put the cooked sausages in buns.
2. For the "fingernail," place a sliver of almond at one end.
3. Drizzling ketchup for a creepy effect is optional..

Nutrition (per finger): ~190 cal | 7g protein | 10g fat | 16g carbs

20. Monster Cheese Quesadillas (Variation)

Cook Time: 10 minutes
Prep Time: 5 minutes
Total Time: 15 minutes

Ingredients:
- 2 large flour tortillas
- 1 cup shredded cheese
- Black olive slices (eyes)
- Salsa (optional)

INSTRUCTIONS:
1. In a pan over medium heat, place the tortilla.
2. Place the second tortilla on top of the shredded cheese.
3. Cook until brown and cheese melts, 2 to 3 minutes per side.
4. Slice the olives for the eyes and cut into triangles.

Nutrition (per serving): ~250 cal | 10g protein | 12g fat | 28g carbs

21. Ghostly Popcorn Balls

Cook Time: 10 minutes
Prep Time: 10 minutes
Total Time: 20 minutes

Ingredients:
- 6 cups popcorn, popped
- ½ cup marshmallows
- 2 tbsp butter
- Mini chocolate chips (for eyes)

INSTRUCTIONS:

1. Over low heat, melt the marshmallows and butter.
2. Add popcorn and stir until covered evenly.
3. While heated, form into little balls.
4. For the ghost eyes, add chocolate chips and allow to cool.

Nutrition (per ball): ~100 cal | 1g protein | 3g fat | 18g carbs

22. Monster Eyeball Cookies

Cook Time: 12 minutes
Prep Time: 10 minutes
Total Time: 22 minutes

Ingredients:
- 1 batch sugar cookie dough
- 12 candy eyeballs
- Icing (optional for decoration)

INSTRUCTIONS:

1. Prepare cookies as directed; let cool.
2. In the center of each biscuit, press a sugar eyeball.
3. If you want more monster detail, apply frosting.

Nutrition (per cookie): ~120 cal | 2g protein | 5g fat | 18g carbs

23. Pumpkin Patch Veggie Cups

Cook Time: 5 minutes
Prep Time: 10 minutes
Total Time: 15 minutes

Ingredients:
- 6 small cups
- 1 cup baby carrots
- ½ cup cherry tomatoes
- Hummus for dipping
- Olive slices (optional for eyes)

INSTRUCTIONS:

1. Pour hummus into cups.
2. Arrange the tomatoes and carrots to resemble little pumpkins.
3. Adding olive slices for frightening faces is optional.

Nutrition (per cup): ~80 cal | 2g protein | 3g fat | 12g carbs

24. Spider Crackers

Cook Time: 5 minutes
Prep Time: 5 minutes
Total Time: 10 minutes

Ingredients:
- 12 round crackers
- 12 small pretzel sticks
- 12 chocolate chips

INSTRUCTIONS:

1. For spider legs, wrap pretzel pieces around crackers.
2. For the spider body, place a chocolate chip in the middle.
3. Serve right away.

Nutrition (per spider): ~60 cal | 1g protein | 2g fat | 10g carbs

25. Jack-o'-Lantern Cheese Balls

Cook Time: 5 minutes
Prep Time: 10 minutes
Total Time: 15 minutes

Ingredients:

- 1 cup shredded cheddar cheese
- 2 tbsp cream cheese
- 6 small cherry tomatoes
- Olive slices for eyes

INSTRUCTIONS:

1. Combine cream cheese and cheddar cheese; form into little balls.
2. Make jack-o'-lantern faces out of slices of tomato and olive.

Nutrition (per ball): ~90 cal | 4g protein | 7g fat | 2g carbs

26. Creepy Cucumber Cups

Cook Time: 5 minutes
Prep Time: 10 minutes
Total Time: 15 minutes

Ingredients:

- 1 cucumber, cut into 1-inch rounds
- 2 tbsp cream cheese
- Olive slices (eyes)

INSTRUCTIONS:

1. Top the cucumber rounds with cream cheese.
2. Slices of olive can be added to make monster eyes.

Nutrition (per cup): ~15 cal | 1g protein | 1g fat | 2g carbs

27. Bat Wings Chicken Nuggets

Cook Time: 15 minutes
Prep Time: 5 minutes
Total Time: 20 minutes

Ingredients:

- 12 chicken nuggets
- 6 small pretzel sticks (wings)

INSTRUCTIONS:

1. As instructed, cook the chicken nuggets.
2. To create the appearance of bat wings, insert pretzel sticks on either side.
3. Warm up and serve.

Nutrition (per serving, 2 nuggets with wings): ~180 cal | 10g protein | 8g fat | 14g carbs

28. Witch Hat Cookies

Cook Time: 12 minutes
Prep Time: 10 minutes
Total Time: 22 minutes

Ingredients:

- 12 chocolate wafer cookies
- 12 chocolate ice cream cones
- ½ cup chocolate frosting
- Sprinkles

INSTRUCTIONS:

1. Spread a dollop of frosting over the wafer cookies that have been placed on the pan.
2. Put an upside-down ice cream cone on each cookie.
3. Sprinkles can be used to create "hat bands."

Nutrition (per cookie): ~120 cal | 2g protein | 5g fat | 18g carbs

29. Monster Veggie Wraps

Cook Time: 5 minutes
Prep Time: 10 minutes
Total Time: 15 minutes

Ingredients:
- 4 large tortillas
- ½ cup cream cheese
- 1 cup shredded carrots and cucumber
- Olive slices for eyes

INSTRUCTIONS:

1. Cover the tortilla with cream cheese.
2. Roll firmly after adding the shredded vegetables.
3. Cut into rounds and garnish with slices of olive for the monster eyes.

Nutrition (per wrap): ~140 cal | 4g protein | 4g fat | 20g carbs

30. Eyeball Deviled Eggs

Cook Time: 10 minutes
Prep Time: 15 minutes
Total Time: 25 minutes

Ingredients:
- 6 hard-boiled eggs
- 3 tbsp mayonnaise
- 1 tsp mustard
- Olive slices (pupils)
- Paprika for garnish

INSTRUCTIONS:

1. Peel and cut the yolks from the eggs.
2. Combine mayo and mustard with the yolks, then add the egg whites back in.
3. To make a "eyeball," place a slice of olive on top of each yolk.
4. For a frightening look, gently sprinkle with paprika.

Nutrition (per egg): ~70 cal | 6g protein | 5g fat | 1g carbs

31. Pumpkin Spice Muffins

Cook Time: 25 minutes
Prep Time: 10 minutes
Total Time: 35 minutes

Ingredients:
- 1 ½ cups all-purpose flour
- 1 tsp baking powder
- ½ tsp baking soda
- 1 tsp pumpkin pie spice
- ½ cup sugar
- 1 cup pumpkin puree
- ½ cup milk
- ¼ cup vegetable oil

INSTRUCTIONS:

1. Turn the oven on to 375°F, or 190°C.
2. In one bowl, combine the dry ingredients; in another, combine the liquid ingredients.
3. Mix both together until smooth.
4. Fill muffin tin; bake for 20 to 25 minutes.

Nutrition (per muffin): ~150 cal | 3g protein | 5g fat | 25g carbs

32. Monster Rice Krispie Treats

Cook Time: 10 minutes
Prep Time: 10 minutes
Total Time: 20 minutes

Ingredients:
- 6 cups Rice Krispies cereal
- 3 tbsp butter
- 1 (10 oz) bag marshmallows
- Green food coloring
- Candy eyes

INSTRUCTIONS:

1. Add green food coloring once the marshmallows and butter have melted.
2. Add cereal and stir until covered.
3. Cool slightly after pressing into the pan.
4. Add candy eyeballs and cut into squares.

Nutrition (per treat): ~150 cal | 2g protein | 4g fat | 28g carbs

33. Mummy Brownies

Cook Time: 25 minutes
Prep Time: 10 minutes
Total Time: 35 minutes

Ingredients:
- 1 box brownie mix
- 1 cup white frosting
- Mini chocolate chips for eyes

INSTRUCTIONS:

1. Bake brownies as directed on the package, then let them cool.
2. To make it look like mummy wrapping, drizzle white icing horizontally.
3. For the eyes, add chocolate chips.

Nutrition (per brownie): ~210 cal | 2g protein | 9g fat | 30g carbs

34. Ghost Banana Smoothies

Cook Time: 5 minutes
Prep Time: 5 minutes
Total Time: 10 minutes

Ingredients:
- 2 bananas
- 1 cup milk
- ½ cup vanilla yogurt
- Mini chocolate chips for ghost eyes

INSTRUCTIONS:

1. Smoothly blend yogurt, milk, and bananas.
2. Transfer to cups and garnish with chocolate chips for the eyes.
3. Serve right away.

Nutrition (per cup): ~120 cal | 3g protein | 2g fat | 25g carbs

35. Eyeball Pasta

Cook Time: 20 minutes
Prep Time: 5 minutes
Total Time: 25 minutes

Ingredients:
- 8 oz spaghetti
- 1 cup marinara sauce
- 4 mozzarella balls
- 4 black olive slices

INSTRUCTIONS:

1. As directed on the package, cook the pasta and then drain it.
2. Toss spaghetti with heated sauce.
3. Top each dish with a mozzarella ball and an olive slice for the "eyeball."

Nutrition (per serving): ~220 cal | 10g protein | 7g fat | 30g carbs

36. Pumpkin Deviled Eggs

Cook Time: 10 minutes
Prep Time: 15 minutes
Total Time: 25 minutes

Ingredients:
- 6 hard-boiled eggs
- 3 tbsp mayonnaise
- 1 tsp mustard
- Paprika
- Chives for stems

INSTRUCTIONS:

1. Peel and cut the yolks from the eggs.
2. Refill the egg whites after mashing the yolks with the mustard and mayo.
3. Add a little bit of chive for the pumpkin stem and sprinkle with paprika.

Nutrition (per egg): ~70 cal | 6g protein | 5g fat | 1g carbs

37. Witch Finger Cookies

Cook Time: 15 minutes
Prep Time: 10 minutes
Total Time: 25 minutes

Ingredients:
- 1 cup butter
- 1 cup sugar
- 1 egg
- 2 cups flour
- 12 almond slices for nails
- Red food gel (optional for blood)

INSTRUCTIONS:

1. Set the oven temperature to 175°C (350°F).
2. To make dough, combine flour, egg, sugar, and butter.
3. Form dough into finger shapes; for nails, press almond pieces.
4. If desired, sprinkle with red gel after baking for 12 to 15 minutes.

Nutrition (per cookie): ~110 cal | 2g protein | 6g fat | 14g carbs

38. Candy Corn Parfaits

Cook Time: 10 minutes
Prep Time: 10 minutes
Total Time: 20 minutes

Ingredients:
- 1 cup vanilla pudding
- 1 cup whipped cream
- Yellow and orange food coloring
- Candy corn

INSTRUCTIONS:

1. Separate the whipped cream and pudding, then tint one half orange and the other yellow.
2. To make it seem like candy corn, layer in transparent cups.
3. Add bits of candy corn on top.

Nutrition (per cup): ~180 cal | 3g protein | 6g fat | 28g carbs

39. Spider Mini Pizzas

Cook Time: 12 minutes
Prep Time: 10 minutes
Total Time: 22 minutes

Ingredients:
- 6 mini pizza bases
- ½ cup pizza sauce
- 1 cup shredded mozzarella
- 12 black olive slices

INSTRUCTIONS:

1. Turn the oven on to 375°F, or 190°C.
2. Top small pizzas with cheese and sauce.
3. Arrange the olives to resemble the body or eyes of spiders.
4. Bake until the cheese melts, 10 to 12 minutes.

Nutrition (per pizza): ~200 cal | 8g protein | 9g fat | 22g carbs

40. Monster Fruit Cups

Cook Time: 5 minutes
Prep Time: 10 minutes
Total Time: 15 minutes

Ingredients:
- 1 cup diced melon, grapes, and berries
- ½ cup yogurt
- Mini chocolate chips for eyes

INSTRUCTIONS:

1. Put fruit in little cups.
2. Add yogurt on top.
3. For the monster eyes, add chocolate chips.

Nutrition (per cup): ~90 cal | 2g protein | 1g fat | 18g carbs

41. Mini Pumpkin Pies

Cook Time: 25 minutes
Prep Time: 10 minutes
Total Time: 35 minutes

Ingredients:
- 6 mini pre-made pie crusts
- 1 cup pumpkin puree
- 2 tbsp sugar
- ½ tsp pumpkin pie spice
- Whipped cream (for topping)

INSTRUCTIONS:

1. Set the oven temperature to 175°C (350°F).
2. Combine sugar, pumpkin spice, and pumpkin puree.
3. Pour mixture into small crusts and bake for 20 to 25 minutes.
4. Before serving, sprinkle whipped cream over top.

Nutrition (per pie): ~150 cal | 2g protein | 5g fat | 22g carbs

42. Spooky Pretzel Sticks

Cook Time: 5 minutes
Prep Time: 5 minutes
Total Time: 10 minutes

Ingredients:
- 12 pretzel rods
- ½ cup white chocolate melts
- Mini chocolate chips for eyes

INSTRUCTIONS:

1. White chocolate that has melted.
2. Place chocolate chips for ghost eyes and dip pretzel points into chocolate.
3. Before serving, let it solidify.

Nutrition (per stick): ~80 cal | 1g protein | 3g fat | 12g carbs

43. Monster Smoothie Bowls

Cook Time: 5 minutes
Prep Time: 10 minutes
Total Time: 15 minutes

Ingredients:
- 1 banana
- ½ cup frozen berries
- ½ cup yogurt
- Granola and fruit for decorating

INSTRUCTIONS:

1. Blend yogurt, banana, and berries until smooth.
2. Transfer to dishes; garnish with fruit and granola to form monster faces.

Nutrition (per bowl): ~150 cal | 4g protein | 2g fat | 30g carbs

44. Witch Hat Brownies

Cook Time: 25 minutes
Prep Time: 10 minutes
Total Time: 35 minutes

Ingredients:
- 1 box brownie mix
- 12 chocolate ice cream cones
- ½ cup frosting
- Sprinkles

INSTRUCTIONS:

1. Cut brownies into squares after baking.
2. Place ice cream cones upside down on each brownie and gently frost the tops.
3. Use sprinkles and frosting to adorn cones.

Nutrition (per brownie hat): ~210 cal | 3g protein | 9g fat | 30g carbs

45. Jack-o'-Lantern Toast

Cook Time: 5 minutes
Prep Time: 5 minutes
Total Time: 10 minutes

Ingredients:
- 4 slices bread
- 2 tbsp cream cheese
- ½ cup shredded cheddar cheese
- Olive slices and red bell pepper for faces

INSTRUCTIONS:

1. Spread cream cheese on the barely toasted bread.
2. Add more cheese and create jack-o'-lantern faces with bell peppers and olives.

Nutrition (per toast): ~160 cal | 6g protein | 8g fat | 15g carbs

46. Spooky Veggie Dip Cups

Cook Time: 5 minutes
Prep Time: 10 minutes
Total Time: 15 minutes

Ingredients:
- 6 small cups
- 1 cup ranch or yogurt dip
- Baby carrots, cucumber sticks, bell pepper strips
- Olive slices (eyes)

INSTRUCTIONS:

1. Pour dip into glasses.
2. Vegetables should be arranged vertically around the cup rim.
3. Add olive slices for eerie monster eyes.

Nutrition (per cup): ~80 cal | 2g protein | 3g fat | 12g carbs

47. Ghostly Cheese Quesadillas

Cook Time: 10 minutes
Prep Time: 5 minutes
Total Time: 15 minutes

Ingredients:
- 2 large tortillas
- 1 cup shredded cheese
- Mini chocolate chips (for ghost eyes)

INSTRUCTIONS:

1. Cook the cheese between the tortillas for two to three minutes on each side, or until it melts.
2. Add chocolate chips for eyes and cut into ghost shapes.

Nutrition (per serving): ~200 cal | 8g protein | 10g fat | 20g carbs

48. Creepy Crawly Trail Mix

Cook Time: 0 minutes
Prep Time: 5 minutes
Total Time: 5 minutes

Ingredients:
- 1 cup cereal
- ½ cup mini pretzels
- ½ cup candy-coated chocolate pieces
- Gummy worms

INSTRUCTIONS:

1. In a large bowl, combine all ingredients.
2. Serve as party favors in individual cups or bags.

Nutrition (per serving, ½ cup): ~120 cal | 2g protein | 2g fat | 24g carbs

49. Spooky Apple Monsters

Cook Time: 10 minutes
Prep Time: 5 minutes
Total Time: 15 minutes

Ingredients:
- 3 apples, cored and sliced into wedges
- Peanut butter or almond butter
- Mini marshmallows (teeth)
- Grape halves (tongue)

INSTRUCTIONS:

1. Spread apple wedges with peanut butter.
2. Put a grape half for the tongue and little marshmallows for the teeth.
3. Serve right away.

Nutrition (per monster): ~100 cal | 2g protein | 3g fat | 18g carbs

50. Bat Wing Chicken Bites

Cook Time: 25 minutes
Prep Time: 5 minutes
Total Time: 30 minutes

Ingredients:
- 1 lb chicken wings or nuggets
- 2 tbsp olive oil
- 1 tsp paprika
- Salt and pepper

INSTRUCTIONS:

1. Turn the oven on to 400°F, or 200°C.
2. Add the paprika, salt, pepper, and olive oil to the chicken.
3. Bake for 20 to 25 minutes, or until well done.

Nutrition (per serving, 4 wings): ~190 cal | 15g protein | 9g fat | 3g carbs

51. Vampire Bite Tacos

Cook Time: 20 minutes
Prep Time: 10 minutes
Total Time: 30 minutes

Ingredients:
- 4 small taco shells
- ½ lb ground beef or turkey
- ½ cup shredded cheese
- ½ cup chopped lettuce
- Salsa

INSTRUCTIONS:

1. Drain extra grease from the skillet after the ground beef is cooked through.
2. Stuff lettuce, cheese, and meat into taco shells.
3. Add salsa on top for a "blood" appearance.

Nutrition (per taco): ~180 cal | 9g protein | 8g fat | 18g carbs

52. Zombie Finger Sandwiches

Cook Time: 15 minutes
Prep Time: 5 minutes
Total Time: 20 minutes

Ingredients:
- 6 slices bread
- 3 tbsp cream cheese
- 6 baby carrots (fingernails)

INSTRUCTIONS:

1. Spread slices of bread with cream cheese, then cut into finger shapes.
2. Put a piece of carrot on the "fingernail" tip.
3. Adding a ketchup dot for blood is optional.

Nutrition (per sandwich): ~120 cal | 3g protein | 4g fat | 16g carbs

53. Haunted Hash Browns

Cook Time: 25 minutes
Prep Time: 5 minutes
Total Time: 30 minutes

Ingredients:

- 2 large potatoes, shredded
- 1 tbsp olive oil
- Salt and pepper
- Ketchup for decoration

INSTRUCTIONS:

1. Turn the oven on to 400°F, or 200°C.
2. Add salt, pepper, and olive oil to the shredded potatoes.
3. Transfer to a baking sheet and bake for 20 to 25 minutes, or until brown.
4. Optional: use ketchup to create eerie designs.

Nutrition (per serving, 1 cup): ~160 cal | 3g protein | 4g fat | 28g carbs

54. Eyeball Spaghetti

Cook Time: 25 minutes
Prep Time: 10 minutes
Total Time: 35 minutes

Ingredients:

- 8 oz spaghetti
- 1 cup marinara sauce
- 4 mozzarella balls
- 4 black olive slices

INSTRUCTIONS:

1. After cooking the spaghetti, drain it.
2. Add spaghetti to heated marinara sauce.
3. Top with mozzarella balls and garnish with slices of olive for "eyeballs."

Nutrition (per serving): ~220 cal | 10g protein | 7g fat | 30g carbs

55. Jack-o'-Lantern Stuffed Peppers

Cook Time: 35 minutes
Prep Time: 10 minutes
Total Time: 45 minutes

Ingredients:

- 4 orange bell peppers
- 1 cup cooked rice
- 1 cup cooked ground turkey or beef
- ½ cup tomato sauce
- Salt and pepper

INSTRUCTIONS:

1. Turn the oven on to 375°F, or 190°C.
2. Slice faces into peppers.
3. Stuff peppers with a mixture of rice, beef, and tomato sauce.
4. Bake for 20 minutes.

Nutrition (per stuffed pepper): ~200 cal | 10g protein | 5g fat | 28g carbs

56. Bat Wing Chicken Bites

Cook Time: 25 minutes
Prep Time: 5 minutes
Total Time: 30 minutes

Ingredients:

- 1 lb chicken wings or nuggets
- 2 tbsp olive oil
- 1 tsp paprika
- Salt and pepper

INSTRUCTIONS:

1. Turn the oven on to 400°F, or 200°C.
2. Add the paprika, salt, pepper, and olive oil to the chicken.
3. Bake for 20 to 25 minutes, or until well done.

Nutrition (per serving, 4 wings): ~190 cal | 15g protein | 9g fat | 3g carbs

57. Spooky Shepherd's Pie

Cook Time: 45 minutes
Prep Time: 10 minutes
Total Time: 55 minutes

Ingredients:

- 1 lb ground beef or turkey
- 1 cup mixed vegetables
- 2 cups mashed potatoes
- Salt and pepper

INSTRUCTIONS:

1. Turn the oven on to 375°F, or 190°C.
2. Season and cook meat with veggies.
3. Cover the meat mixture with mashed potatoes after layering it in the baking dish.
4. Bake until golden, 20 to 25 minutes.

Nutrition (per serving): ~280 cal | 14g protein | 12g fat | 28g carbs

58. Eyeball Pizza

Cook Time: 15 minutes
Prep Time: 10 minutes
Total Time: 25 minutes

Ingredients:

- 1 pre-made pizza crust
- ½ cup pizza sauce
- 1 cup shredded mozzarella
- 6 olive slices for "eyeballs"

INSTRUCTIONS:

1. Turn the oven on to 375°F, or 190°C.
2. Cover the crust with sauce and top with cheese.
3. To make it seem like eyeballs, add olives.
4. Bake until the cheese melts, 12 to 15 minutes.

Nutrition (per slice, 1/6 pizza): ~200 cal | 8g protein | 9g fat | 22g carbs

59. Monster Macaroni Bake

Cook Time: 30 minutes
Prep Time: 10 minutes
Total Time: 40 minutes

Ingredients:

- 3 cups cooked macaroni
- 2 cups shredded cheddar
- 1 cup milk
- 2 tbsp butter

INSTRUCTIONS:

1. Set the oven temperature to 175°C (350°F).
2. In a baking dish, combine the macaroni, cheese, milk, and butter.
3. Add more cheese on top and bake for 15 to 20 minutes.

Nutrition (per serving): ~250 cal | 12g protein | 10g fat | 28g carbs

60. Ghostly Tomato Soup

Cook Time: 25 minutes
Prep Time: 5 minutes
Total Time: 30 minutes

Ingredients:

- 4 cups tomato puree
- 1 cup vegetable broth
- ½ tsp garlic powder
- ½ cup milk
- Mini croutons

INSTRUCTIONS:

1. Put the broth, tomato puree, and garlic powder in a saucepan and let it boil.
2. Add milk and stir.
3. Serve with little ghost-shaped croutons.

Nutrition (per serving): ~90 cal | 3g protein | 3g fat | 14g carbs

61. Spider Web Pancakes

Cook Time: 10 minutes
Prep Time: 5 minutes
Total Time: 15 minutes

Ingredients:
- 1 cup pancake mix
- ¾ cup milk
- 1 egg
- 2 tbsp chocolate syrup

INSTRUCTIONS:

1. Add the egg and milk to the pancake batter.
2. Pancakes should be cooked over medium heat in a skillet.
3. Drag a toothpick outward to create a web design after pouring chocolate syrup in concentric rings.

Nutrition (per pancake): ~120 cal | 3g protein | 3g fat | 22g carbs

62. Mummy Calzones

Cook Time: 20 minutes
Prep Time: 10 minutes
Total Time: 30 minutes

Ingredients:
- 1 package pizza dough
- ½ cup pizza sauce
- 1 cup shredded mozzarella
- Black olive slices for eyes

INSTRUCTIONS:

1. Turn the oven on to 375°F, or 190°C.
2. Roll out the dough, stuff it with cheese and sauce, then fold and seal the edges.
3. Top with sliced pieces to make it seem like mummy wrap.
4. Add olive slices for the eyes and bake for 15 to 20 minutes.

Nutrition (per calzone): ~250 cal | 10g protein | 9g fat | 30g carbs

63. Pumpkin Pancakes

Cook Time: 10 minutes
Prep Time: 5 minutes
Total Time: 15 minutes

Ingredients:
- 1 cup pancake mix
- ½ cup pumpkin puree
- ¾ cup milk
- 1 tsp pumpkin pie spice

INSTRUCTIONS:

1. Blend all the items until they are smooth.
2. Cook till brown in a non-stick skillet.
3. Serve with whipped cream or syrup after stacking.

Nutrition (per pancake): ~130 cal | 3g protein | 3g fat | 23g carbs

64. Monster Cheese Toasties

Cook Time: 5 minutes
Prep Time: 5 minutes
Total Time: 10 minutes

Ingredients:
- 4 slices bread
- ½ cup shredded cheddar cheese
- Olive slices for eyes

INSTRUCTIONS:

1. Sandwich two pieces of bread with cheese, then melt it on the grill.
2. Place slices of olive oil on top to create monster eyes.

Nutrition (per toastie): ~180 cal | 7g protein | 8g fat | 18g carbs

65. Ghostly Pudding Cups

Cook Time: 5 minutes
Prep Time: 5 minutes
Total Time: 10 minutes

Ingredients:
- 2 cups vanilla pudding
- Mini chocolate chips for eyes

INSTRUCTIONS:

1. Fill cups with pudding.
2. For ghost eyes, add chocolate chips.
3. Before serving, let it cool for ten minutes.

Nutrition (per cup): ~120 cal | 3g protein | 2g fat | 22g carbs

66. Witch's Cauldron Chili

Cook Time: 30 minutes
Prep Time: 10 minutes
Total Time: 40 minutes

Ingredients:
- 1 lb ground beef or turkey
- 1 can kidney beans, drained
- 1 can diced tomatoes
- 1 tsp chili powder
- Salt and pepper

INSTRUCTIONS:

1. In a saucepan, cook the meat until browned.
2. Add the chili powder, tomatoes, beans, salt, and pepper.
3. Serve hot after 20 minutes of simmering.

Nutrition (per serving, 1 cup): ~200 cal | 12g protein | 7g fat | 18g carbs

67. Candy Corn Rice Krispie Treats

Cook Time: 10 minutes
Prep Time: 10 minutes
Total Time: 20 minutes

Ingredients:
- 6 cups Rice Krispies cereal
- 3 tbsp butter
- 1 (10 oz) bag marshmallows
- Yellow and orange food coloring

INSTRUCTIONS:

1. Melt marshmallows with butter, then separate and tint sections with orange and yellow.
2. To make it seem like candy corn, arrange colorful marshmallows on top of cereal.
3. Cool after pressing into the pan, then cut into triangles.

Nutrition (per piece): ~150 cal | 2g protein | 4g fat | 28g carbs

68. Monster Veggie Skewers

Cook Time: 5 minutes
Prep Time: 10 minutes
Total Time: 15 minutes

Ingredients:
- 12 cherry tomatoes
- 12 cucumber slices
- 12 mini mozzarella balls
- Toothpicks

INSTRUCTIONS:

1. Each toothpick should include a single ball of mozzarella, cucumber, and tomato.
2. Adding an olive slice for eyes is optional.

Nutrition (per skewer): ~35 cal | 2g protein | 1g fat | 5g carbs

69. Ghostly Garlic Bread

Cook Time: 10 minutes
Prep Time: 5 minutes
Total Time: 15 minutes

Ingredients:
- 1 baguette, sliced
- 2 tbsp butter
- 1 tsp garlic powder
- Mini black olive slices

INSTRUCTIONS:

1. Set the oven temperature to 175°C (350°F).
2. Spread bread slices with a mixture of garlic powder and butter.
3. Add olive slices to create ghost faces after 8 to 10 minutes of baking.

Nutrition (per slice): ~80 cal | 2g protein | 3g fat | 12g carbs

70. Pumpkin Spice Smoothie

Cook Time: 5 minutes
Prep Time: 5 minutes
Total Time: 10 minutes

Ingredients:
- ½ cup pumpkin puree
- 1 banana
- ½ cup milk
- ¼ tsp pumpkin pie spice

INSTRUCTIONS:

1. Blend each item until it's smooth.
2. Serve in tiny glasses right away.

Nutrition (per serving): ~100 cal | 2g protein | 1g fat | 22g carbs

71. Monster Nachos

Cook Time: 10 minutes
Prep Time: 5 minutes
Total Time: 15 minutes

Ingredients:
- 6 corn tortilla chips
- ½ cup shredded cheddar cheese
- 2 tbsp salsa
- 6 black olive slices (eyes)

INSTRUCTIONS:

1. Set the oven temperature to 175°C (350°F).
2. Place the chips on a baking dish and top them with cheese.
3. Bake until the cheese melts, 5 to 7 minutes.
4. Drizzle salsa and add olive slices for monster eyes.

Nutrition (per serving): ~150 cal | 6g protein | 7g fat | 18g carbs

72. Witch Finger Pretzels

Cook Time: 10 minutes
Prep Time: 5 minutes
Total Time: 15 minutes

Ingredients:
- 12 pretzel rods
- 12 almond slices (fingernails)
- ¼ cup white chocolate melts

INSTRUCTIONS:

1. Dip the tip of the pretzels in melted white chocolate.
2. For the fingernail, press a sliver of almond onto the chocolate.
3. Before serving, let it set.

Nutrition (per pretzel): ~80 cal | 1g protein | 3g fat | 12g carbs

73. Pumpkin Rice Pudding

Cook Time: 25 minutes
Prep Time: 5 minutes
Total Time: 30 minutes

Ingredients:
- 1 cup cooked rice
- 1 cup milk
- ¼ cup sugar
- ½ cup pumpkin puree
- ½ tsp pumpkin spice

INSTRUCTIONS:

1. In a saucepan, combine milk, sugar, pumpkin puree, and pumpkin spice.
2. Add the cooked rice and boil until it thickens, 15 to 20 minutes.
3. Serve hot or cold.

Nutrition (per cup): ~150 cal | 3g protein | 3g fat | 28g carbs

74. Monster Apple Pops

Cook Time: 5 minutes
Prep Time: 10 minutes
Total Time: 15 minutes

Ingredients:
- 3 apples, sliced into wedges
- 3 tbsp peanut butter
- Mini marshmallows
- Grape halves

INSTRUCTIONS:

1. Spread apple wedges with peanut butter.
2. Put a grape half for the tongue and little marshmallows for the teeth.
3. If a pop effect is desired, insert a stick.

Nutrition (per pop): ~100 cal | 2g protein | 3g fat | 18g carbs

75. Ghostly Donuts

Cook Time: 15 minutes
Prep Time: 5 minutes
Total Time: 20 minutes

Ingredients:
- 6 mini plain donuts
- ½ cup white frosting
- Mini chocolate chips for eyes

INSTRUCTIONS:

1. Use white icing to coat the donuts.
2. For ghost eyes, add chocolate chips.
3. Serve right away or refrigerate for a little.

Nutrition (per donut): ~150 cal | 3g protein | 5g fat | 24g carbs

76. Spooky Jello Cups

Cook Time: 10 minutes (plus chilling)
Prep Time: 5 minutes
Total Time: 1 hour

Ingredients:
- 1 package lime or orange gelatin
- 1 cup boiling water
- 1 cup cold water
- Gummy worms

INSTRUCTIONS:

1. Add cold water after dissolving the gelatin in hot water.
2. Pour into cups and refrigerate for 45 to 60 minutes or until firm.
3. Put gummy worms inside or on top.

Nutrition (per cup): ~90 cal | 1g protein | 0g fat | 22g carbs

77. Candy Corn Parfaits

Cook Time: 10 minutes
Prep Time: 5 minutes
Total Time: 15 minutes

Ingredients:
- 1 cup vanilla pudding
- 1 cup whipped cream
- ½ cup crushed yellow cake or cookie crumbs
- Candy corn

INSTRUCTIONS:

1. In cups, arrange the cake crumbs, pudding, and whipped cream.
2. Add candy corn on top.
3. Serve cold.

Nutrition (per cup): ~180 cal | 3g protein | 6g fat | 28g carbs

78. Mini Jack-o'-Lantern Pies

Cook Time: 35 minutes
Prep Time: 10 minutes
Total Time: 45 minutes

Ingredients:
- 6 mini pre-made pie crusts
- 1 cup pumpkin puree
- 2 tbsp sugar
- ½ tsp pumpkin pie spice
- Whipped cream

INSTRUCTIONS:

1. Fill pie crusts with a mixture of pumpkin, sugar, and spice.
2. Bake for 20 to 25 minutes at 350°F (175°C).
3. Before serving, sprinkle whipped cream over top.

Nutrition (per mini pie): ~150 cal | 2g protein | 5g fat | 22g carbs

79. Spooky Halloween Cake Pops

Cook Time: 30 minutes
Prep Time: 10 minutes
Total Time: 40 minutes

Ingredients:
- 2 cups crumbled cake
- ½ cup frosting
- 12 candy melts (white, orange, black)
- Lollipop sticks

INSTRUCTIONS:

1. Combine frosting and cake crumbs; shape into balls.
2. Put in the sticks and chill for ten minutes.
3. Add Halloween faces as decorations and dip in candy melts.

Nutrition (per cake pop): ~130 cal | 2g protein | 5g fat | 18g carbs

80. Graveyard Dirt Cups

Cook Time: 10 minutes
Prep Time: 5 minutes
Total Time: 15 minutes

Ingredients:
- 6 chocolate pudding cups
- ½ cup crushed chocolate cookies
- 6 cookie tombstones (store-bought or homemade)
- Gummy worms

INSTRUCTIONS:

1. For "dirt," sprinkle smashed cookies over the pudding.
2. Put in a cookie gravestone.
3. Add the crawling gummy worms.

Nutrition (per cup): ~180 cal | 3g protein | 6g fat | 28g carbs

81. Spiderweb Taco Dip

Cook Time: 5 minutes
Prep Time: 10 minutes
Total Time: 15 minutes

Ingredients:
- 1 cup refried beans
- ½ cup sour cream
- ½ cup shredded cheddar cheese
- Black olives (for spider)

INSTRUCTIONS:

1. Spread a small plate with refried beans.
2. Create a spiderweb design by dragging a toothpick outward after pipetting the sour cream in concentric circles.
3. Add sliced olives for spider and sprinkle with cheddar cheese.

Nutrition (per serving): ~120 cal | 4g protein | 6g fat | 12g carbs

82. Monster Cupcakes

Cook Time: 20 minutes
Prep Time: 10 minutes
Total Time: 30 minutes

Ingredients:
- 1 box chocolate or vanilla cupcake mix
- 1 cup frosting
- Candy eyes
- Sprinkles

INSTRUCTIONS:

1. As directed on the package, bake the cupcakes and allow them to cool.
2. Frost cupcakes and create monster faces with sprinkles and candy eyes.

Nutrition (per cupcake): ~180 cal | 2g protein | 7g fat | 28g carbs

83. Ghostly Cheese Balls

Cook Time: 5 minutes
Prep Time: 10 minutes
Total Time: 15 minutes

Ingredients:
- 1 cup shredded cheddar cheese
- 2 tbsp cream cheese
- Mini black olives (for eyes)

INSTRUCTIONS:

1. Combine cream cheese and cheddar cheese; form into little ghost shapes.
2. For the eyes, add little olives.

Nutrition (per cheese ball): ~90 cal | 4g protein | 7g fat | 2g carbs

84. Pumpkin Pie Smoothie

Cook Time: 5 minutes
Prep Time: 5 minutes
Total Time: 10 minutes

Ingredients:
- ½ cup pumpkin puree
- 1 banana
- ½ cup milk
- ¼ tsp pumpkin pie spice

INSTRUCTIONS:

1. Blend each item until it's smooth.
2. Serve in tiny glasses right away.

Nutrition (per serving): ~100 cal | 2g protein | 1g fat | 22g carbs

85. Mummy Cheese Sticks

Cook Time: 10 minutes
Prep Time: 5 minutes
Total Time: 15 minutes

Ingredients:
- 6 string cheese sticks
- 6 crescent roll dough strips
- Mini chocolate chips (for eyes)

INSTRUCTIONS:

1. To make it seem like mummy, wrap crescent roll dough over string cheese.
2. Bake at 375°F (190°C) for 8 to 10 minutes.
3. For the eyes, add chocolate chips.

Nutrition (per stick): ~150 cal | 7g protein | 7g fat | 14g carbs

86. Witch Hat Cupcakes

Cook Time: 20 minutes
Prep Time: 10 minutes
Total Time: 30 minutes

Ingredients:
- 1 box cupcake mix
- 12 chocolate ice cream cones
- Frosting and sprinkles

INSTRUCTIONS:

1. As directed, bake the cupcakes.
2. Place chocolate cones upside down on each cupcake and frost the tops.
3. For the hat bands, decorate with icing and sprinkles.

Nutrition (per cupcake): ~180 cal | 2g protein | 7g fat | 28g carbs

87. Pumpkin Cheesecake Bites

Cook Time: 25 minutes
Prep Time: 10 minutes
Total Time: 35 minutes

Ingredients:
- 1 cup cream cheese
- ½ cup pumpkin puree
- 2 tbsp sugar
- ½ tsp pumpkin spice
- Mini graham cracker crusts

INSTRUCTIONS:

1. Blend the sugar, spice, pumpkin, and cream cheese until creamy.
2. Fill little graham cracker crusts with the mixture using a spoon.
3. Before serving, let it cool for 20 minutes.

Nutrition (per bite): ~120 cal | 3g protein | 7g fat | 10g carbs

88. Creepy Crawly Trail Mix

Cook Time: 0 minutes
Prep Time: 5 minutes
Total Time: 5 minutes

Ingredients:
- 1 cup cereal
- ½ cup pretzels
- ½ cup candy-coated chocolates
- Gummy worms

INSTRUCTIONS:

1. In a large bowl, combine all ingredients.
2. Serve in separate bags or mugs.

Nutrition (per serving, ½ cup): ~120 cal | 2g protein | 2g fat | 24g carbs

89. Eyeball Punch

Cook Time: 5 minutes
Prep Time: 5 minutes
Total Time: 10 minutes

Ingredients:
- 4 cups fruit punch
- 1 cup lychee (canned, drained)
- Blueberries (for eyeball center)

INSTRUCTIONS:

1. Fill a big bowl with punch.
2. Put the blueberry into the lychee to make it seem like floating eyeballs.

Nutrition (per cup): ~70 cal | 1g protein | 0g fat | 18g carbs

90. Monster Fruit Kabobs

Cook Time: 5 minutes
Prep Time: 10 minutes
Total Time: 15 minutes

Ingredients:
- 12 grapes
- 12 melon balls
- 12 cubes pineapple
- Toothpicks
- Mini chocolate chips for eyes

INSTRUCTIONS:

1. Fun combinations of fruit may be threaded onto toothpicks.
2. Make monster eyes out of chocolate chips on pineapple or melon balls.

Nutrition (per kabob): ~50 cal | 1g protein | 0g fat | 13g carbs

91. Vampire Cupcakes

Cook Time: 20 minutes
Prep Time: 10 minutes
Total Time: 30 minutes

Ingredients:
- 1 box chocolate cupcake mix
- 1 cup red frosting
- Candy fangs or almond slices
- Mini chocolate chips

INSTRUCTIONS:

1. As directed, bake the cupcakes and allow them to cool.
2. Use crimson frosting to make it seem like "blood."
3. For eyes, add chocolate chips and sugar fangs.

Nutrition (per cupcake): ~180 cal | 2g protein | 7g fat | 28g carbs

92. Mummy Pretzel Rods

Cook Time: 5 minutes
Prep Time: 10 minutes
Total Time: 15 minutes

Ingredients:
- 12 pretzel rods
- ½ cup white chocolate melts
- Mini chocolate chips for eyes

INSTRUCTIONS:

1. Drizzle melted white chocolate in a zigzag pattern over pretzel sticks.
2. Add mummy eyes chocolate chips.
3. Before serving, let it set.

Nutrition (per rod): ~80 cal | 1g protein | 3g fat | 12g carbs

93. Eyeball Pancakes

Cook Time: 10 minutes
Prep Time: 5 minutes
Total Time: 15 minutes

Ingredients:
- 1 cup pancake mix
- ¾ cup milk
- 1 egg
- 6 mozzarella balls
- 6 black olive slices

INSTRUCTIONS:

1. As directed on the package, prepare the pancakes.
2. Place a mozzarella ball and a black olive slice on top of each pancake to create a "eyeball."

Nutrition (per pancake): ~120 cal | 3g protein | 3g fat | 22g carbs

94. Ghostly Marshmallow Pops

Cook Time: 5 minutes
Prep Time: 10 minutes
Total Time: 15 minutes

Ingredients:
- 12 large marshmallows
- ½ cup white chocolate melts
- Mini chocolate chips for eyes
- Lollipop sticks

INSTRUCTIONS:

1. Put sticks inside marshmallows.
2. Add chocolate chips for the eyes after dipping in melted white chocolate.
3. Before serving, let it set.

Nutrition (per pop): ~80 cal | 1g protein | 2g fat | 15g carbs

95. Jack-o'-Lantern Quesadillas

Cook Time: 10 minutes
Prep Time: 5 minutes
Total Time: 15 minutes

Ingredients:
- 2 large tortillas
- 1 cup shredded cheddar cheese
- Olive slices and bell pepper pieces for faces

INSTRUCTIONS:

1. Top one tortilla with cheese, then the other tortilla.
2. Cook until the cheese melts, 2 to 3 minutes per side.
3. Cut into triangles and create jack-o'-lantern faces with peppers and olives.

Nutrition (per quesadilla): ~200 cal | 8g protein | 10g fat | 20g carbs

96. Witch's Brew Smoothie

Cook Time: 5 minutes
Prep Time: 5 minutes
Total Time: 10 minutes

Ingredients:
- 1 cup spinach
- 1 banana
- ½ cup pineapple
- ½ cup orange juice

INSTRUCTIONS:

1. Blend each item until it's smooth.
2. Serve in little glasses, and feel free to garnish with gummy worms.

Nutrition (per serving): ~90 cal | 2g protein | 0g fat | 22g carbs

97. Monster Cheese Crackers

Cook Time: 5 minutes
Prep Time: 5 minutes
Total Time: 10 minutes

Ingredients:
- 12 crackers
- ½ cup cream cheese
- Olive slices for eyes
- Sliced peppers for mouths

INSTRUCTIONS:

1. Spread crackers with cream cheese.
2. To make monster faces, add peppers and olive slices.

Nutrition (per cracker): ~60 cal | 2g protein | 3g fat | 6g carbs

98. Pumpkin Patch Cupcakes

Cook Time: 20 minutes
Prep Time: 10 minutes
Total Time: 30 minutes

Ingredients:
- 1 box cupcake mix
- 1 cup orange frosting
- Green licorice for stems
- Mini chocolate chips for eyes

INSTRUCTIONS:

1. Cool after baking the cupcakes.
2. Cover with orange frosting; decorate with chocolate chips and licorice stems for faces.

Nutrition (per cupcake): ~180 cal | 2g protein | 7g fat | 28g carbs

99. Ghostly Fruit Cups

Cook Time: 5 minutes
Prep Time: 5 minutes
Total Time: 10 minutes

Ingredients:
- 1 cup diced melon, grapes, and berries
- ½ cup yogurt
- Mini chocolate chips for eyes

INSTRUCTIONS:

1. Put fruit in cups.
2. Add chocolate chips for ghost eyes and yogurt on top.

Nutrition (per cup): ~90 cal | 2g protein | 1g fat | 18g carbs

100. Graveyard Chocolate Pudding

Cook Time: 5 minutes
Prep Time: 5 minutes
Total Time: 10 minutes

Ingredients:
- 2 cups chocolate pudding
- ½ cup crushed chocolate cookies
- Gummy worms
- Cookie tombstones

INSTRUCTIONS:

1. Fill cups with pudding.
2. For soil, sprinkle smashed cookies on top.
3. Add gummy worms and cookie tombstones.

Nutrition (per cup): ~180 cal | 3g protein | 6g fat | 28g carbs

Printed in Dunstable, United Kingdom